Sally's new shoes

Annette Smith
Illustrated by Meredith Thomas

I'm going to walk
in my new shoes.

I'm going to run
in my new shoes.

I'm going to jump in my new shoes.

I'm going to hop
in my new shoes.

I'm going to climb
in my new shoes.

I'm going to dance
in my new shoes.

But I'm not going to ...

... **swim**

in my new shoes!